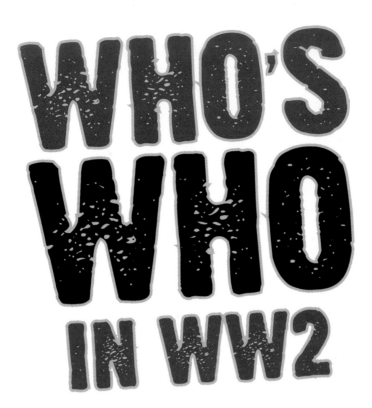

WHO'S WHO IN WW2

Alison Hawes

Published 2011
First published in hardback 2010 by
A&C Black Publishers Ltd.
36 Soho Square, London, W1D 3QY

www.acblack.com

ISBN 978-1-4081-2679-0

Series consultant: Gill Matthews

Text copyright © 2010 Alison Hawes

The author would like to thank Ruth Foster, whose testimony about her girlhood experiences of Nazi persecution can be heard in the Holocaust Exhibition at the Imperial War Museum, and Hazel Brown of the IWM for invaluable help and advice.

Produced for A&C Black by Calcium. www.calciumcreative.co.uk

Printed and bound in China by C&C Offset Printing Co.

All the internet addresses given in this book were correct at the time of going to press. The author and publishers regret any inconvenience caused if addresses have changed or sites have ceased to exist, but can accept no responsibility for any such changes.

Acknowledgements

The publishers would like to thank the following for their kind permission to reproduce their photographs:

Cover: Corbis: Bettmann bl, background, Keystone r. **Pages:** Alamy Images: Photos 12 22; Imperial War Museum and Step Haiselden: 26; Istockphoto: Jaap2 10; Library of Congress: 5b, 6, 18, 25, Elias Goldensky 9; National Archives and Records Administration: 5t, 13b, 19, 20, 28, 29t; Rex Features: 14, 15, 16, Caters News Agency Ltd 23; Shutterstock: BESTWEB 11, Gary Blakeley 24; U.S. Air Force: 12; Wikimedia Commons: 7, 17, 21, Acmthompson 8, Japanese Library of Parliament Digital Archive 13t, United States Department of Energy 29b, Wisnia6522 27.

Contents

A World at War

World War II (1939-1945) was the biggest, most destructive war ever. By its end, at least 55 million men, women, and children were dead and millions more were left injured or homeless.

Axis v Allies

The war was fought between the **Axis Powers**, led by Germany and Japan, and the **Allies**, led by Britain, America, and the **Soviet Union**.

The Axis	The Allies	
Germany	Britain	America
Japan	Soviet Union	France
Italy	Poland	Canada
	Australia	India
	New Zealand	China
	Norway	and many more...
	South Africa	

Human suffering

Millions of people on both sides of the war suffered horribly during World War II. For the first time in any war to date more **civilians** than **military** were killed.

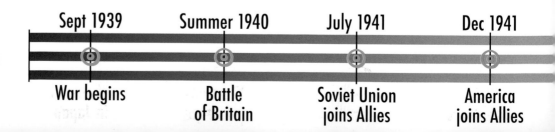

Sept 1939	Summer 1940	July 1941	Dec 1941
War begins	Battle of Britain	Soviet Union joins Allies	America joins Allies

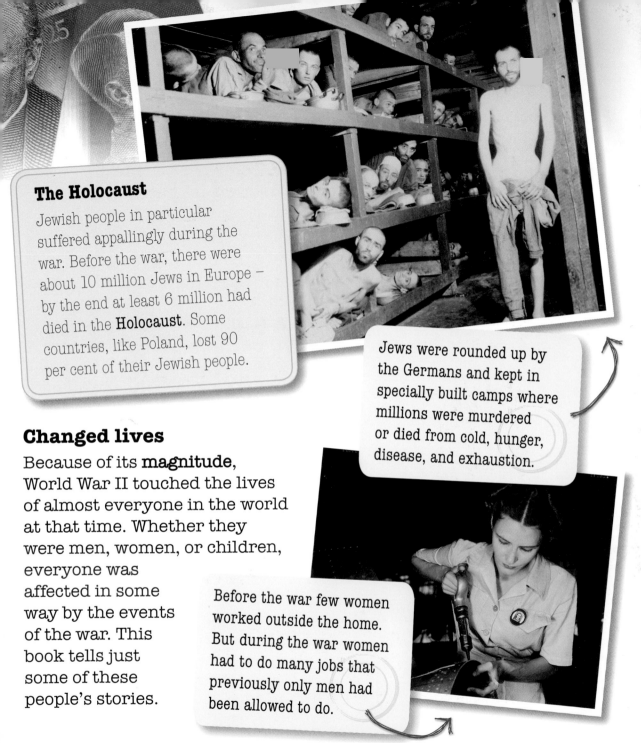

The Holocaust

Jewish people in particular suffered appallingly during the war. Before the war, there were about 10 million Jews in Europe – by the end at least 6 million had died in the **Holocaust**. Some countries, like Poland, lost 90 per cent of their Jewish people.

Jews were rounded up by the Germans and kept in specially built camps where millions were murdered or died from cold, hunger, disease, and exhaustion.

Changed lives

Because of its **magnitude**, World War II touched the lives of almost everyone in the world at that time. Whether they were men, women, or children, everyone was affected in some way by the events of the war. This book tells just some of these people's stories.

Before the war few women worked outside the home. But during the war women had to do many jobs that previously only men had been allowed to do.

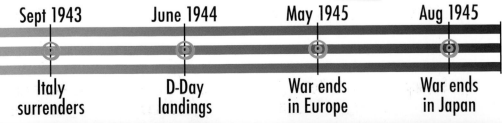

Sept 1943	June 1944	May 1945	Aug 1945
Italy surrenders	D-Day landings	War ends in Europe	War ends in Japan

Adolf Hitler

Adolf Hitler moved to Germany to join the army at the outbreak of the First World War. He liked the army and was devastated when Germany lost the war.

Nazi Party

After the end of the war, Hitler joined a group called the German Worker's Party. It later became the **Nazi** party. With Hitler as its leader, the party grew more powerful until it had won many seats in parliament and Hitler became **Chancellor** of Germany.

Hitler often spoke at large political rallies. He was a very persuasive and powerful speech maker.

Racists

Hitler and his party were racists who believed that people of pure Germanic blood were superior (better) to every other race. In particular, they were fiercely anti-Jewish. When Hitler came to power, life became increasingly dangerous for Jews and anyone else his party considered "inferior".

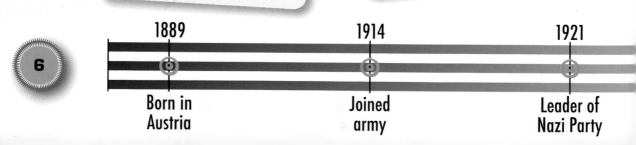

1889	1914	1921
Born in Austria	Joined army	Leader of Nazi Party

World War II

As Chancellor, Hitler built up the German military and began to seize land from neighbouring countries. When he attacked Poland in 1939, Britain and France declared war on Germany and the war began.

The end

By 1941, much of Europe was under Hitler's control. But then Hitler made the mistake of attacking the Soviet Union. This was a fight he would not win. When it was clear that Germany had lost the war, Hitler committed **suicide**.

Once in power, Hitler began arresting Jews and sending them to **concentration camps**.

Did you know?

ADOLF HITLER

- It is thought Hitler was a vegetarian.
- He only became a German citizen the year before he became Chancellor.

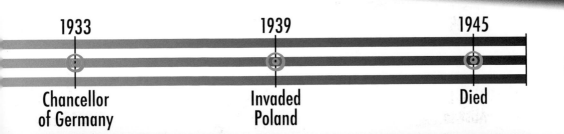

1933
Chancellor of Germany

1939
Invaded Poland

1945
Died

Oskar Schindler

Oskar Schindler (1908–1974) was a member of the Nazi party. He became a hero to hundreds of Jews in World War II.

Making money

When World War II broke out, Schindler went to Poland where he became rich making goods for the German army. Many of his factory workers were Jewish and Schindler realized that the Nazis planned to kill them.

Saving lives

Using his friendship with the Nazis and his money to pay huge **bribes**, Schindler prevented hundreds of his workers from being sent to the **gas chambers**.

Unforgettable rescuer

By the end of the war, Schindler was almost penniless. But those he rescued never forgot him and when he died they paid for him to be buried in Israel, where many of them now live.

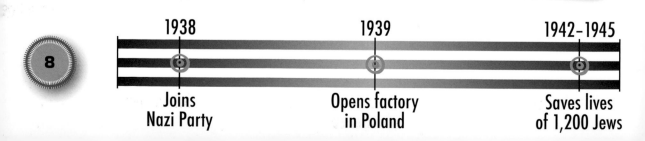

1938	1939	1942–1945
Joins Nazi Party	Opens factory in Poland	Saves lives of 1,200 Jews

Franklin D. Roosevelt

Nationality:
American

Franklin Roosevelt had been a successful politician for ten years when he suddenly fell seriously ill with polio. **As a result of this he had to use a wheelchair for the rest of his life. But, undeterred, Franklin returned to politics and became president for the first time in 1932.**

Franklin Roosevelt (1882–1945) is the only American president, to be elected to office four times!

Attacked

At the start of World War II, Roosevelt was determined to keep America out of the war. But in 1941, Japan attacked the American Navy, which left Roosevelt no option but to go to war. With America on their side, the Allies were confident they would win the war. But Roosevelt did not live to see this. He died three weeks before Germany surrendered.

Did you know?

FRANKLIN D. ROOSEVELT

• Roosevelt helped create the United Nations, to help avoid wars in the future.

1921	1932	1941
Ill with polio	President of America	Enters War

9

Anne Frank

Until she was four, Anne Frank was just an ordinary little girl. But in 1933, Hitler came to power in Germany and soon Jewish families like Anne's were no longer safe.

Anne's diary shows us what life was like for many Jewish children in World War II.

Into hiding

When Anne was thirteen, the Germans started rounding up the Jews where she lived and sending them to concentration camps. Anne and her family hid in a secret **annexe** in the building where her father's business was based.

Betrayed!

After two long years in hiding, someone betrayed the Franks. Police burst into the annexe and arrested them. In the confusion, Anne's diary was left behind.

1929	1933	1942
Born in Germany	Moved to the Netherlands	Started her diary in June

Anne's diary

Anne dreamt of being a writer and while she was in hiding, she kept a diary of her thoughts and feelings. She explained how the family had to keep still and quiet during the day, as people still worked in the building where they were hiding. One wrong move and someone might hear them and give them away to the Germans.

This statue of Anne Frank in Amsterdam stands in front of the building where she hid.

The end

The family was sent to various concentration camps but Anne's father was the only one to survive. Anne died from **typhus** just weeks before the end of the war. She was fifteen years old. She would never know that her diary would be found and published and her dream of becoming a famous writer would come true.

Did you know?

ANNE FRANK

• Anne is short for Annelies.
• The diary was a present for her thirteenth birthday.

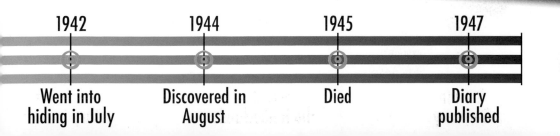

1942	1944	1945	1947
Went into hiding in July	Discovered in August	Died	Diary published

Alan Turing

**Alan Turing (1912–1954) was a member
of a secret army of men and women who
helped the Allies win World War II.**

Code cracker

During the war, Turing
worked as a code breaker.
His job was to **decode**
German military radio
messages so the Allies
could find out what the
enemy was planning to
do next. But the code was
complicated and almost
impossible to crack.

Over 200 Bombe
machines were used
during the war.

Did you know?

ALAN TURING

- The Turing Bombe was an early
  type of computer.
- After the war, Turing worked on
  developing his ideas for computers.

The Bombe

Then Turing and his
team designed a machine
that could do millions of
calculations faster than
any person. With the help
of these huge machines,
called Bombes, the code
was cracked. But Turing's
work was so secret few
people knew about it until
years after the war.

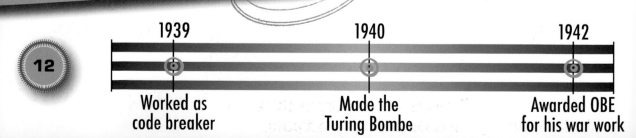

1939	1940	1942
Worked as code breaker	Made the Turing Bombe	Awarded OBE for his war work

Hideki Tojo

As a young man, Tojo (1884-1948) became a soldier and was quickly promoted. But he was also interested in politics and later became Prime Minister of Japan.

World War II

Tojo wanted to help Japan become a large, powerful country by seizing land from its neighbouring countries. But the Allies, who had many interests in the area, were against this. So in 1941, after Japan attacked the American Navy, they declared war on Japan.

Tojo was Minister of War as well as Prime Minister.

Allied prisoners held by the Japanese celebrate the end of the war.

War Criminal

The Japanese were fierce fighters and at first the war went Japan's way. But in 1944, when it looked like Japan would be defeated, Hideki resigned as Prime Minister. After the war, he was found guilty of war crimes and was hanged in 1948.

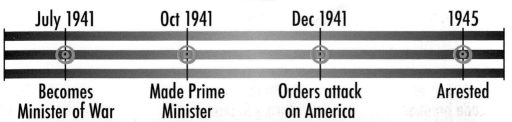

July 1941	Oct 1941	Dec 1941	1945
Becomes Minister of War	Made Prime Minister	Orders attack on America	Arrested

13

Douglas Bader

In World War II, Britain's best-known pilot was Douglas Bader.

Crash landing

When he was eighteen, Douglas Bader trained as a pilot with the RAF. He was a very skilful pilot – but was not so good at obeying orders! This eventually got him into real trouble. On 14th December 1931, ignoring orders not to fly his plane at very low **altitude**, he crashed. He lost both his legs. Although Bader learned to walk – and even fly – with the aid of artificial limbs, he was devastated when he had to leave the RAF.

As a boy, Bader went to stay with his uncle, who worked for the RAF. It was then that Bader decided he wanted to be a pilot.

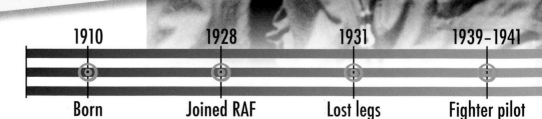

1910	1928	1931	1939–1941
Born	Joined RAF	Lost legs	Fighter pilot in RAF

RAF pilots like Bader flew Spitfires and Hurricanes during World War II.

Champion of disabled

After the war, Bader left the RAF and went to work in the **aviation industry**. He also helped to inspire and raise money for people who were disabled like him. He became Sir Douglas Bader in 1976 when the Queen awarded him a **knighthood** for his work with the disabled.

Ace pilot

When World War II began, Bader badgered the RAF into letting him fly again. He proved to be a brilliant fighter pilot, shooting down at least 22 enemy aircraft. But on 9 August 1941, his plane was shot down over France and he was made a prisoner of war (POW). Bader tried to escape so often, the Germans threatened to take away his artificial legs! In the end, he was sent to **Colditz Castle** until the end of the war.

Did you know?

DOUGLAS BADER

- Bader's nickname was Dogsbody.
- Two pubs have been named after him.

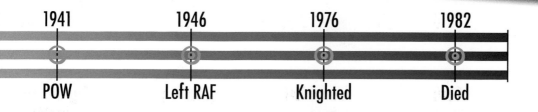

1941	1946	1976	1982
POW	Left RAF	Knighted	Died

Violette Szabo

In World War II, Violette Szabo (1921–1945) worked as a secret agent for the Allies.

A secret life

When Szabo's husband was killed in the war, she wanted to help with the war effort in some way. So when she was asked to train as a secret agent, she jumped at the chance. But she couldn't tell anyone what she was doing.

Into danger

Szabo was parachuted into France to help the French. They wanted to cause as much damage and disruption as they could to the German forces **occupying** their country. If she was stopped by the enemy, Szabo pretended she was a French businesswoman.

Captured!

During Szabo's second mission, she was captured and tortured by the Germans. She refused to give the enemy any information and was sent to a concentration camp. Months later, she was shot dead.

Szabo could speak both French and English.

1943	April 1944	June 1944	Dec 1946
Trained as Secret agent	First mission	Second mission	Awarded George cross

Chiune Sugihara

In World War II, Chiune Sugihara (1900–1986) was the Japanese diplomat **in Lithuania. Here, he helped thousands of Jews escape the Nazis. He issued them with** visas **to travel to a safe country, even though the Japanese government said he was not to do this.**

A difficult decision

Sugihara knew the Jews would be killed if he didn't help them escape. But he didn't want to defy his government either. In the end, he decided to help the **refugees**.

Race against time

For weeks Sugihara and his wife worked round the clock issuing visas. They helped over 6,000 Jews to escape to safety before they were forced to leave the country themselves.

The only way Jews could avoid capture was to hide or to leave Europe.

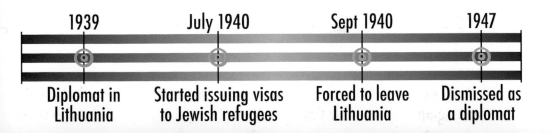

1939	July 1940	Sept 1940	1947
Diplomat in Lithuania	Started issuing visas to Jewish refugees	Forced to leave Lithuania	Dismissed as a diplomat

Winston Churchill

Winston Churchill was the prime minister who led Britain to victory in World War II.

Member of Parliament

After leaving school, Churchill joined the British Army. He enjoyed life as a soldier but left to become an MP (Member of Parliament), like his father.

Prime Minister

A few months after World War II broke out, Prime Minister Neville Chamberlain resigned. Churchill took his place. The war was not going well for the Allies. Germany had invaded much of Western Europe and Britain soon came under almost daily attack from German and Italian bombers.

Winston Churchill was an MP for over sixty years.

1874	1900	1908
Born	MP	Married

Between 1940 and 1941, Britain suffered severe bombing known as the Blitz.

After the war

Within a month of winning the war in Europe, Churchill was replaced as Prime Minister. He remained an MP though, and eventually became Prime Minister again during the 1950s. He finally retired as an MP in 1964. He died the following year. His funeral was watched on television by millions of people.

No surrender!

Many British cities were heavily bombed. Churchill made **numerous**, brilliant speeches to parliament and on the radio. He urged the people of Britain not to give up, despite the bombing, and never to surrender. Churchill was seen as a national hero for the way he led his country during this time.

Did you know?

WINSTON CHURCHILL

- Winston Churchill was a gifted writer.
- When Churchill first became an MP it was not a paid job, so he earned money by writing.
- Churchill was good at bricklaying and painting.

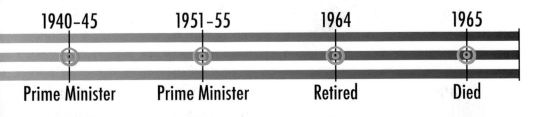

1940–45	1951–55	1964	1965
Prime Minister	Prime Minister	Retired	Died

Vernon J. Baker

Vernon Baker (born 1919) is the only living black World War II soldier to be awarded the Medal of Honor.

Segregated

When Baker first joined the army, it was as part of an all black **unit**. This was because there was prejudice against black people in America at the time and black and white people were often **segregated**.

After the war

When segregation ended, Baker became one of the first black officers to be put in charge of an all white **company**.

Heroism

In World War II, Baker led an attack against the Germans. Because of Baker's **heroism**, many enemy soldiers were killed and several machine guns were captured. He was not rewarded for his bravery until over fifty years later because of the prejudice against black Americans at the time.

Like the Army, the US Navy was segregated for many years.

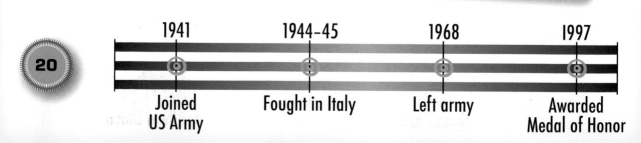

1941	1944–45	1968	1997
Joined US Army	Fought in Italy	Left army	Awarded Medal of Honor

Lydia Litvyak

In World War II, women were rarely allowed to fight. But Soviet pilot Lydia Litvyak (1921-1943) was an exception.

Fighter pilot

Litvyak became a flying instructor but she wanted to be a fighter pilot. Then in 1942 she was allowed to join the Soviet Air Force. She became a very successful pilot, shooting down many enemy aircraft. But in August 1943, Litvyak and her plane disappeared.

Missing

For a long time no one knew what had happened to Litvyak. But years later a plane with a body inside was found. It was Litvyak. She was given a state funeral and made a Hero of the Soviet Union, almost fifty years after she died.

Litvyak was fifteen when she first flew a plane on her own.

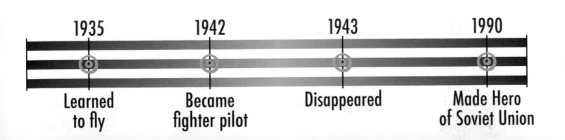

1935	1942	1943	1990
Learned to fly	Became fighter pilot	Disappeared	Made Hero of Soviet Union

Roger Bushell

During World War II, millions of people were taken prisoner. Like Roger Bushell, many believed it was their duty to escape.

Shot down

During the war, Bushell flew **Spitfires**. But in May 1940, his plane was shot down over France and he was captured and sent to a **POW camp**. Bushell escaped twice but was eventually recaptured each time.

Tom, Dick, and Harry

After his second escape, Bushell was put in one of the most secure POW camps the Germans had. Here, Bushell was put in charge of the escape committee. Before long, the committee had drawn up plans for 200 prisoners to tunnel their way out. Work soon began on three secret tunnels – called Tom, Dick, and Harry!

Roger Bushell's story was made into a famous film called *The Great Escape*.

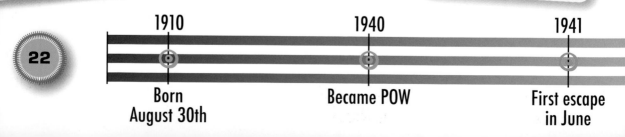

1910	1940	1941
Born August 30th	Became POW	First escape in June

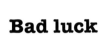

Bad luck

Everything was going well until "Tom" was discovered by the prison guards and "Dick" became unusable. On 24 March 1944, "Harry" was finally ready. The "Great Escape" was about to begin when it was discovered that the tunnel was 3 metres (10 ft) short of the woods. This was where the prisoners had hoped to exit, undetected.

A sketch of the POW camp where the Great Escape took place.

The great escape

The committee decided to go ahead and 76 prisoners, including Bushell, managed to escape before a prison guard found the tunnel exit. All but three men were recaptured. Fifty of them, including Bushell, were shot dead on the orders of Hitler.

Did you know?

ROGER BUSHELL

• Bushell was an excellent skier.
• He spoke French and German fluently.

1941	1944	1944
Second escape in October	Third escape in March	Died

Frank Partridge

Frank Partridge (1924-1964) was the youngest Australian to win the Victoria Cross in World War II.

Nationality:
Australian

Called up

When he was 18, Partidge joined the Australian army and fought for the Allies against the Japanese.

182 Victoria Crosses were awarded during the war. 20 of them went to Australians.

Hero

In 1945, Partidge's bravery earned him the Victoria Cross. His unit was trying to destroy an enemy position, when Partridge came under fire. Despite being hit by three bullets, Partridge took out one enemy position and attacked another, until he was finally forced to stop because he had lost so much blood.

Life after the war

After the war, Partridge went back to work on his father's farm. In 1963, he married and had a baby son. Tragically, Partridge died in a car accident the following year.

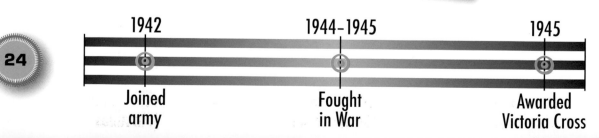

1942	1944-1945	1945
Joined army	Fought in War	Awarded Victoria Cross

Joseph Stalin

Joseph Stalin (1879-1953) became the leader of the Soviet Union in the 1920s. For many years, he ruled the Soviet people through fear - killing or imprisoning many of those who opposed him.

Stalin's last name was Dzhugashvili, but he called himself Stalin, meaning "steel".

Changing sides

At the start of World War II, Stalin and Hitler made a deal, promising not to attack each other. But two years later, Hitler broke this promise and attacked the Soviet Union, so Stalin changed sides and joined the Allies.

Winning the war

Stalin's soldiers helped push Hitler's army out of the countries it had occupied in Europe. This helped the Allies win the war, but it meant much of Eastern Europe would remain under Soviet control long after Stalin's death in 1953.

Did you know?

JOSEPH STALIN

• Of the 55 million who died in World War II 20 million came from the Soviet Union alone.

1939	1941	1941
Made pact with Hitler	Hitler attacks Soviet Union	Soviet Union join Allies

Ruth Foster

**Nationality:
German**

Millions of Jews perished in World War II. A few, like Ruth Foster, miraculously survived.

Deported

In 1941, Ruth and her parents were **deported** from Germany to **Riga**. For two years, Ruth lived behind the barbed wire of the Riga **ghetto**. There was barely enough food to survive and cruelty and death were never far away.

Killings

Prisoners who worked outside the ghetto during the day smuggled in extra food if they could. When Ruth's father was caught doing this, he was shot dead in front of her. Later the ghetto was closed and Ruth and her mother were taken to a nearby concentration camp. Ruth's mother was killed soon afterwards.

Ruth survived life in a Nazi concentration camp.

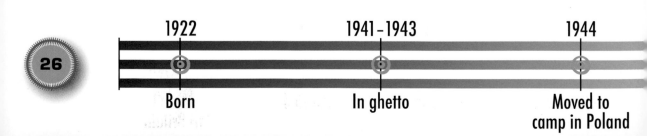

1922	1941–1943	1944
Born	In ghetto	Moved to camp in Poland

Death march

In 1945, the Germans forced Ruth and her fellow prisoners to march by night for weeks on end. Finally, the Allies caught up with them and she was rescued. By this time, Ruth was alive, but only just. Very weak and ill with typhus, Ruth was twenty two, but weighed less than a seven-year-old.

Ruth eventually recovered and moved to the UK in 1947, where she still lives.

Gas chambers

In July 1944, Ruth was moved to the Stutthof camp in Poland. On arrival, she was taken to the gas chambers. But Ruth didn't die. By an amazing stroke of luck the camp had run out of poison gas.

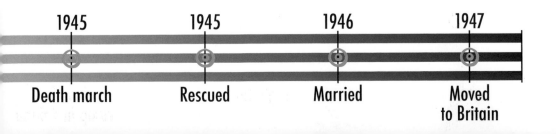

1945	1945	1946	1947
Death march	Rescued	Married	Moved to Britain

Benito Mussolini

As a young man, Benito Mussolini (1883–1945) involved himself in politics, eventually becoming Prime Minister of Italy. By 1926 he had banned all political parties but his own. Then he began to invade countries nearby, with the aim of building a new Italian Empire.

Hitler's friend

During World War II, Mussolini fought on Hitler's side. But the war did not go well for Mussolini and his troops. So, in 1943, he was sacked as Prime Minister. Mussolini was imprisoned and, not long after Italy surrendered to the Allies.

The end

The Germans rescued Mussolini and fought on in Italy. But as the Allies gradually took control of Italy, Mussolini tried to escape to Switzerland. He was caught and shot by his countrymen on 28 April 1945.

Mussolini introduced anti-Jewish laws in Italy, as Hitler had done in Germany.

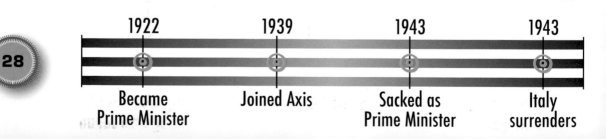

1922	1939	1943	1943
Became Prime Minister	Joined Axis	Sacked as Prime Minister	Italy surrenders

Robert Oppenheimer

Nationality:
American

Robert Oppenheimer (1904–1967) was a brilliant scientist who helped develop one of the world's deadliest weapons.

Secret project

During World War II, Oppenheimer was put in charge of a highly secret project – to make an atomic bomb before the Germans did! It took him just three years to do it.

The Gadget

When the bomb (code-named the Gadget) was tested, the flash from the explosion was seen 250 miles away. Every living thing within a mile of it was dead.

Ending the war

By now the war against Germany was over but the Japanese refused to surrender. So the Americans used the bomb against the Japanese to end the war.

Oppenheimer loved science but could also speak many languages.

Thousands of people died when two bombs were dropped on Japan.

1942–45	July 1945	August 1945
Worked on the Gadget	Bomb tested	Bomb used against Japan

29

Glossary

Allies countries led by Britain, France, the USA and the Soviet Union, that fought against the Axis powers in World War II

altitude height above the ground

annexe small separate building

aviation industry work to do with aircraft

Axis Powers countries who fought with Germany in World War II

bribes money paid to someone to persuade them to do what you want

chancellor head of government

civilians ordinary citizens, not people in the armed forces

Colditz Castle high security German prison that was hard to escape from

company group of soldiers headed by a captain

concentration camps places where Jews and other people the Nazis persecuted were held prisoner

decode to work out a code

deported to be sent by force to another country

diplomat official who represents his country abroad

gas chambers specially built rooms where people were gassed to death

ghetto part of a city where people the Germans persecuted had to live

heroism extreme bravery

Holocaust mass murder of the Jews by the Nazis in World War II

knighthood special award from the Queen, making someone a Sir

magnitude largeness

military armed forces

Nazi German political party led by Adolf Hitler

numerous many, lots of

occupying when one country takes over another by force

polio infectious disease that can leave someone paralyzed

POW camp place where prisoners of war were held

refugees people searching for safety by moving to another country

Riga capital city of Latvia

segregated when different racial groups are separated by law

Soviet Union Russia and the surrounding countries

Spitfires fighter planes used in the Battle of Britain

suicide to kill oneself on purpose

typhus infectious fever

unit group of soldiers that train and work together

visas documents or stamps in passports, allowing people to leave or enter another country

Further Information

Websites

Discover background information and animations about World War II at:

www.nationalarchives.gov.uk/education/worldwar2

Read biographies of important people from history at:

www.bbc.co.uk/history/historic_figures

Books

The Second World War by Henry Brook.
Usbourne (2009).

True Stories of the Second World War
by P. Dowswell. Usborne (2007).

World War II Newsletter
by Paul Mason. A&C Black (2010).

Museums

Imperial War Museum
Lambeth Road, London
www.iwm.org.uk

Churchill Museum and Cabinet War Rooms
King Charles Street, London
www.iwm.org.uk

Imperial War Museum
Duxford, Cambridgeshire
duxford.iwm.org.uk

Imperial War Museum North
Trafford Park Warehouse
Manchester
north.iwm.org.uk

Index

BETTWS 13|5|1,